D1017218

THE 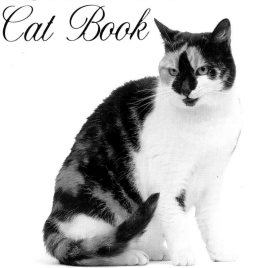 LITTLE
CALICO &
TORTOISESHELL
Cat Book

DAVID TAYLOR

DAPHNE NEGUS
Consulting Editor

SIMON AND SCHUSTER
New York • London • Toronto • Sydney • Tokyo • Singapore

A DORLING KINDERSLEY BOOK

SIMON AND SCHUSTER
Simon & Schuster Building
Rockefeller Center
1230 Avenue of the Americas
New York, New York 10020

Simultaneously published in Great Britain
by Dorling Kindersley Limited,
9 Henrietta Street, London WC2E 8PS

PROJECT EDITOR Corinne Hall
PROJECT ART EDITOR Nigel Hazle
MANAGING ART EDITOR Nick Harris
MANAGING EDITOR Vicky Davenport

Printed in Italy by Mondadori

1 3 5 7 9 10 8 6 4 2

Library of Congress Catalog Card Number: 90-32241 [tk]
ISBN: 0 - 671 - 70987 - 9

CONTENTS

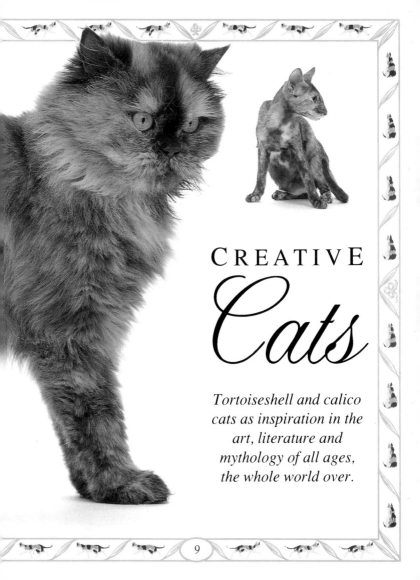

CREATIVE
Cats

Tortoiseshell and calico cats as inspiration in the art, literature and mythology of all ages, the whole world over.

FANTASY AND FOLKLORE

Tortoiseshell and calico cats have often featured in fantasy and folklore. Here are some fascinating felines.

Tortoiseshell and calico cats are thought to be lucky in many parts of the world. In England, they bring good luck, and anyone playing with a tortoiseshell or calico kitten could gain the gift of second sight. These cats could predict the future and, in France, a calico or tortoiseshell seen climbing a tree signified that someone would die violently.

SCOTTISH MYTHS

Households in Scotland welcomed them in, believing that they brought good health to all the family. However, should anyone become ill, they were obliged to wash themselves and throw the remaining dirty water over the household cat.

The drenched cat, chased out of doors, would obligingly take the illness with her. If, however, she left the house of her own accord, the sick person would then be certain to die.

TORTOISESHELL TOUCH

Anyone in the home who suffered from warts could be cured by stroking the afflicted area with the tip of a tortoiseshell cat's tail. Unfortunately, this remedy was only effective during the month of May. Kittens born in May, however, were thought to be unlucky and were suspected of bringing snakes and worms indoors, which would then suffocate babies.

Left: Desirable Domestic Companion; Right: Tortoiseshell Toddler; Below right: Prime Viewing Position.

Tortoiseshells were always welcomed on board ship, as they brought good fortune to the vessel and protected her entire crew.

SEA CATS

In the Far East, sailors would, tradition tells us, hoist their ship's resident tortoiseshell to the top of the mast, where she could scare off storm devils. If a Greek sailor was misguided enough to throw a cat into the ocean, a storm was then absolutely certain to follow.

A cat running crazily up and down the deck was also thought to be a warning of rough weather ahead.

FELINE FORECAST

The ship's cat was always one of the first to be saved if the vessel was wrecked. Another useful cat talent was weather prediction: a sneeze or furious scratching behind the ear meant rain in the offing; a cat warming its back by the fire indicated frost on the way; a sleeping cat with its paws over its nose foretold gales to come.

TORTOISESHELL & CALICO CAT FACTS

Cats are fascinating creatures. Here are some tantalizing tortoiseshell and calico cat facts to delight cat lovers.

Tortoiseshell and calico cats are a puzzle to naturalists and, even nowadays, producing a calico or tortoiseshell kitten is really more a matter of chance than experienced kitten-planning. The various complexities of feline genetics governing color mean that almost all these cats are female. Every now and then, through a genetic hiccup, a male kitten appears in a litter, but he is almost always sterile.

ORIENTAL TORTIE

Tortoiseshell and calico cats have always been more common in the Orient than elsewhere, and probably originated in Asia Minor. Their scarcity makes them lucky talismans.

This is especially so in Japan, where tortoiseshells and calicos are rarities, considered to possess certain magical powers.

FLYING FELIX

Felix, a pretty calico cat, was flown from Frankfurt to Los Angeles, where he was going to join his owners. Felix managed to break out of his traveling cage and was duly reported missing. In fact he was still in the hold and he survived in the aircraft without either food or water. Twenty-nine days, sixty-four flights and 179,900 miles later, the globe-trotting puss was returned to his bemused but delighted owners in America.

*Far Left: Curiosity and the Calico Cat;
Above: At the Feet of the Egyptian Master;
Right: Pensive Tortoiseshell Puss.*

13

HALL OF FELINE FAME

Here are some tortoiseshell and calico cats that have graced the corridors of feline fame in art and literature.

George Stubbs, the eighteenth-century British artist best known for his superb paintings of horses, produced his only study in oils of a cat in a painting of a charming tortoiseshell-and-white kitten which belonged to a friend. The only other time a cat appeared in his paintings was when he featured one alongside a horse known as The Godolphin Arabian. The cat had been the horse's lifelong friend. When the stallion died, his faithful companion kept watch by the body, before dying of grief.

PARISIAN PUSS

Few artists have specialized in painting cats so prolifically as FrenchmanTheophile Steinlen.

At the end of the nineteenth century, he turned out feline pictures by the hundreds. His Parisian studio was particularly well-located for the artist to observe French street cats.

LOVING FELINE

The reclusive British artist Gwen John, eclipsed during her lifetime by her larger-than-life brother Augustus, relied heavily on her pet tortoiseshell cat for company. She sketched the cat who, although female, was named Edgar Quinet, after the street in Paris where Gwen John lived, and was utterly heartbroken when, one day, her pet strayed away from home and was lost, never again to return.

CHIC CAT

The writer William Cowper, a favourite of Jane Austen, acquired a kitten and wrote to his cousin: "I have a kitten, my dear, the drollest of all creatures that ever wore a cat's skin... she is dress'd in a tortoiseshell suit and I know that you will delight in her."

Far Left: Tea-Time Tortoiseshell;
Above: Tortoiseshell Kitten in Oils;
Left: Steinlein's Parisian Poster Pussycats.

GALLERY OF
Cats

A sumptuous and select portrait gallery of calico and tortoiseshell cats - from luscious pedigree Persian to friendly family cat.

FELINE FEATURES

Every cat's features are uniquely expressive of its innermost character. Breeding often shows itself most obviously in the face, and especially in the eyes, the windows of the soul, which are also monitors of the slightest changes in mood, health or well-being. An alert, sparkling, interested cat is a joy to behold, as any cat lover will agree.

OSWALD
Tortoiseshell Persian

DOROTHY
Tortoiseshell-and-White Rumpy Manx

CAMILLA
Calico Shorthair

FLEUR
British Tortoiseshell Shorthair

JESSICA
Tortoiseshell Persian

SAMMY
Oriental Tortoiseshell Shorthair

TRIXIE
Non-pedigree

FLORENCE
Non-pedigree

CALICO SHORTHAIR

Dressed to kill in a wonderful, flowing coat of many colors, this cat is particularly delightful in kittenhood. Patches of creamy ginger, blue and white mingle in the silky fur. These cats are nearly always female, with a calm, charming disposition.

CATERISTICS

❦

Always unruffled and serene.

❦

Very outgoing.

❦

Loves making friends.

FLUFFY FEATURES

These cats have solid, rounded bodies draped with luxuriant fur, tails that are bushy, and small, delicately tufted ears.

SHOW CAT

The Calico Shorthair is a relatively new variety and is making many appearances at shows.

Random Factor

The colors in the coat should be random, but fairly even, with no one shade predominating. A patch of cream or white on the face is a sought-after feature, which emphasizes the dark, penetrating copper eyes.

BRITISH TORTOISESHELL SHORTHAIR

Britain was the first country to establish a breed standard for shorthaired cats, hence the British Shorthair. Its robust, chunky build and rounded, comfortable outline have made it a favored domestic cat and home companion. A British Tortoiseshell Shorthair is, however, surprisingly hard to breed, due to the peculiarities of the tortoiseshell gene.

COZY CAT

The British Shorthair has short, well-proportioned legs, with large round paws and a resilient, compact body which is an absolute delight to hug.

PURR-FECT PROFILE

The British Shorthair profile is admirably demonstrated here: the round, broad face with short, straight nose, an even bite and well-defined chin are all desirable features in a top-ranking cat of this breed.

CATERISTICS

🐾

A luxury-loving cat.

🐾

A cat that loves people.

🐾

A calm, affectionate, domestic companion.

PILLOW CAT

The ultimate lap cat, this particular feline has a well-developed taste for luxury in life. She returns the love and affection bestowed on her by her owners by warming their pillows for them!

CAMEO PERSIAN

The sumptuous coat of the Cameo Persian is deliciously dappled and creamy. This is because tortoiseshell colors are confined to the tips of each hair, while the main length of the hair is white. The color takes on a different intensity depending on the length of the colored tip - in some cats, the effect is of a glimmer of color against a misty white background.

TIP-TOP COAT
The fur is thick, silky and luxurious. The areas of darkest color appear on the broad face, along the back and on the sturdy legs and large paws.

CATERISTICS
❦
An easy-going animal,
not in the least bit
temperamental.

❦
Fond of sensuous
pleasures.

❦
Delights in
being pampered!

TAIL END
The Cameo Persian is justifiably proud
of its coat, and carries its thickly furred tail
straight and low, rarely curling it upward.

SUITABLY RUFFLED
A splendid neck ruff frames this cat's stunning, owl-like,
firm-chinned face. The ears are small, round-tipped
and tufted, the eyes large, brilliant copper discs.

TORTOISESHELL MANX

Meet the cat whose tail, it is said, was caught in the door of Noah's Ark! Or perhaps it swam ashore from the wrecked ships of the Spanish Armada, arriving on the remote Isle of Man, midway between Britain and Ireland. Whatever the truth, this breed has become closely identified with the island, where it features on coins and stamps. Oddly enough, the lack of a tail doesn't appear to affect the cat's balance. It has exceptionally long hind legs, which give it tremendous spring and speed.

WHAT A TALE

A true Manx has nothing but a hollow at the base of the spine, or sometimes a little tuft of fur where the tail would have been.

DANGEROUS GENE
When tail-less Manx
cats are mated, their
genes often produce
defects and the
kittens die.

STRANGE NAMES
Manx cats with no tail at all
are called "Rumpies"; some
sport the remnant of a tail and
are called "Risers",
"Stubbies" or "Longies",
according to the length of
the tail.

CATERISTICS

An amicable cat.

Affectionate
and lovable.

Loves the rough-and-
tumble of family life.

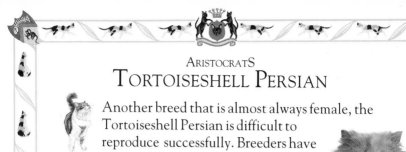

TORTOISESHELL PERSIAN

Another breed that is almost always female, the Tortoiseshell Persian is difficult to reproduce successfully. Breeders have tried various combinations of parentage, but the mix of black, cream and red can be difficult to capture. The long hair diffuses the patches of color, which should be clearly defined and even. The ears also should have broken color, and a blaze of cream or red on the face is a bonus for a potential show cat.

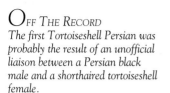

OFF THE RECORD
The first Tortoiseshell Persian was probably the result of an unofficial liaison between a Persian black male and a shorthaired tortoiseshell female.

OWL OR PUSSY CAT?
This cat has an extraordinary round, flattened face, made even more owl-like by the small ears, lengthy ear tufts and gleaming copper orbs.

CATERISTICS
🐱
An excellent mother, taking great care of her kittens.

🐱
Docile and gentle.

🐱
A particularly loving nature.

SOFT TOUCH
Superbly rumpled, the fur is thick and feels sensuously silky to the touch. The tail is short, and majestically plumed.

ORIENTAL TORTOISESHELL

This sleek, proud breed was developed by crossing Siamese cats with other shorthaired types to produce a cat with an elegant, exotic appearance and a beautifully patterned coat. Here, the tortoiseshell coloring is a mixture of patches and blotches. The body is typically lithe and athletic, with slender legs and a long tail that tapers down to a fine point.

Facially, the cat is very much like a Siamese, with an imperious gaze and widely spaced, bewitchingly green eyes.

SVELTE AND SILKY

The coat lies close to the cat's body, and the fur is short with a fine, silky texture. Although these cats are very active, they love spending time on their owners' laps. They are very loving and can form strong bonds with people.

CATERISTICS

🐈

A cat of distinction that
enjoys attracting attention.

🐈

An expansive personality
with plenty of charm.

🐈

Energetic and vigorous.

INQUISITIVE
In temperament, the
Oriental has inherited
all the energy and
curiosity of the
Siamese.

THEMATIC VARIATION
Well-known varieties of the
Oriental Shorthair are the
Chestnut, and the pitch-black Ebony.

TRIXIE

Trixie, a stray who was given to her owners, is a wonderful example of a non-pedigree calico cat: black, cream and red appear on a pure white background. The genetic make-up of female felines allows them to mix orange/red and black and display the result as tortoiseshell; the tortoiseshell tom cat is not the creature of myth he is held to be, but only rarely crops up in a litter and is invariably sterile.

MIRROR IMAGE
Trixie's fine-featured face, complete with long, white whiskers and eyebrows, is delightfully blotched with creamy ginger and black.

CATERISTICS

🐾

Affectionate but not immediately at ease with strangers.

🐾

Likes outdoor adventuring.

🐾

A reserved and dignified cat.

PATCHWORK PET

The soft, short, evenly patched coat is highly individual in its coloring and easy to care for. The pretty white socks are kept scrupulously neat and clean by their owner!

STARRY EYES

The pea-green eyes and ginger-tipped ears lend an air of intelligent curiosity to this "typical Gemini" cat.

FAMILY FRIENDS
FLORENCE

Florence is a well-built cat whose trace of British Shorthair blood demonstrates itself in her short, dense fur and robust frame. The British Shorthair legacy also endows her with a sweet temperament: by no means neurotic, this disposition makes for the ideal family companion and friend, loving and supremely adaptable to circumstance.

COZY PAD

The coat, evenly and generously sprinkled with black, cream and red, is slightly more dense than is usual because Florence lives outside. She sleeps on a raised, heated pad with her loving male companion, Dougal.

BRITISH BUILD
The legs and short,
blunt tail are distinctly
those of the British
Shorthair, as are the
large, padded feet.

CATERISTICS

Not in the least
neurotic.

Independent but
loving nature.

The ideal
household pet.

CREAM SILK
The delightfully alert, round face
and amber eyes are beautifully
set off by a fetching, soft,
creamy blaze on the throat.
The slightly flat nose may
indicate Persian blood.

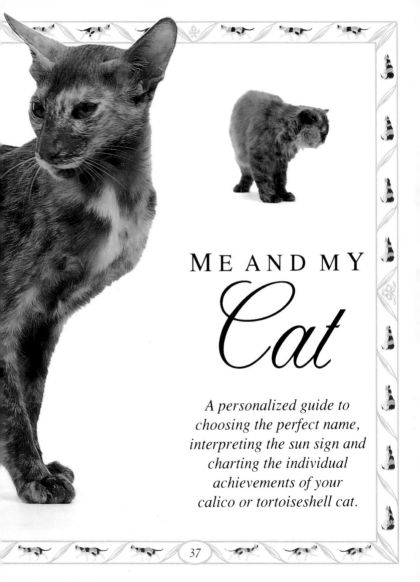

ME AND MY
Cat

A personalized guide to choosing the perfect name, interpreting the sun sign and charting the individual achievements of your calico or tortoiseshell cat.

MY CAT'S PURR-SONAL HISTORY

My cat's name ....

Date of birth ....

Birthplace ....

Weight ....

Sun sign ....

Color of eyes ....

Color of coat ....

Distinguishing features ....

Mother and father (if known) ....

Brothers and sisters ....

MY CAT'S FAVORITE THINGS

Gastronomic goodies ....

Napping spots ....

Cat-tricks and games ....

Special stroking zones ....

Main scratching post ....

THE FIRST TIME MY CAT…

Opened its eyes ....

Drank a saucer of milk ....

Ate solid food ....

Sat on my lap and purred ....

Said "Meow!" properly ....

Understood the point of kitty litter ....

Presented its first mouse-gift ....

Got stuck in a tree ....

Tried to climb into the bathtub.......................................

Met a strange cat ....

Fell in love ....

Ran up the curtains ....

Saw a dog ....

Smelled catnip ....

Used body language ....

Used the cat-flap ....

Went exploring outdoors ....

NAMES AND NAMING

"The Naming of Cats is a difficult matter," wrote T. S. Eliot in *Old Possum's Book of Practical Cats*. He didn't make it any easier by suggesting that cats should have "three different names": one "the family use daily", one that's "more dignified", and one known only to the cat, a "deep and inscrutable, singular Name". Nevertheless, the following suggestions may solve the problem for you!

AMISH *An American sect that live a simple, rural life and specialize in making superb patchwork quilts.*

BUTTERFLY *In honor of the tortoiseshell butterfly, which, like its feline namesake, bears marvelous blotched markings.*

CALICO *The perfect name for a puss whose coat bears striking resemblance to calico print material.*

CHINTZIE *Tortoiseshell-and-white cats are sometimes called chintz cats in Britain.*

CHRYSANTHEMUM *Flower of Japan, a country where tortoiseshell and calico cats are treated with particular respect and courtesy.*

GWEN *After the reclusive artist Gwen John, much given to painting her beloved tortoiseshell cat.*

HARLEQUIN *Especially suitable for a cat with black around the eyes, resembling the mask worn by Columbine's sad lover.*

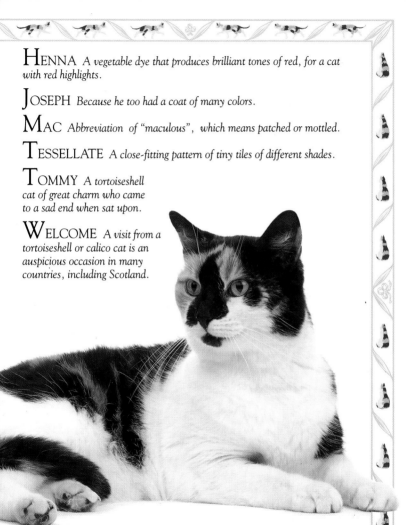

H ENNA *A vegetable dye that produces brilliant tones of red, for a cat with red highlights.*

J OSEPH *Because he too had a coat of many colors.*

M AC *Abbreviation of "maculous", which means patched or mottled.*

T ESSELLATE *A close-fitting pattern of tiny tiles of different shades.*

T OMMY *A tortoiseshell cat of great charm who came to a sad end when sat upon.*

W ELCOME *A visit from a tortoiseshell or calico cat is an auspicious occasion in many countries, including Scotland.*

CAT SUN SIGNS

Check out your cat's sun sign and pick a compatible pet.

ARIES
MARCH 21 - APRIL 20

Adventurous creatures, Aries cats are not restful pets. Although fiercely independent, they have a very loyal streak, and adore being fussed over when in the right mood. *LIBRAN owners lavish attention on the egocentric Aries cat; AQUARIAN owners like the Aries cat's straightforward approach to life.*

TAURUS
APRIL 21 - MAY 21

The Taurean puss is always purring and is happiest when asleep on its favorite bed. Taureans love food and, not surprisingly, tend to be rather plump. Placid and easy-going, they react fiercely if angered. *VIRGOAN owners create the home Taurean cats love; PISCEAN owners are relaxed by Taurean cats.*

GEMINI
MAY 22 - JUNE 21

An out-and-about cat that gets restless if expected to be a constant, lap-loving companion. An incurable flirt, the Gemini cat's lively nature makes for fascinating, sometimes exasperating, company. *SAGITTARIAN owners share the Gemini cat's need for challenge; VIRGOAN owners won't restrict Gemini cats.*

Cancer
JUNE 22 - JULY 22

Ideal for someone who spends a lot of time at home, the Cancer cat will be constantly at your side, climbing on to your lap at every opportunity. But tread carefully: Cancer cats are easily offended. CAPRICORN *owners suit the Cancer cat's desire for stability;* TAUREAN *owners give Cancer cats security.*

Leo
JULY 23 - AUGUST 23

King or queen of the household, Leo cats must rule the roost unchallenged. They have a striking appearance and keep their coats in shape. They adore praise and will go out of their way to attract attention. CANCER *owners like Leo cats taking charge;* ARIAN *owners enjoy the Leo cat's acrobatics.*

Virgo
AUGUST 24 - SEPTEMBER 22

"Take no risks" is this cat's motto. Intelligent thinkers, Virgoan cats don't mind if their owner is out all day and love a change of scene or a trip in the cat basket. SCORPIO *owners complement the Virgoan cat's inquisitive nature;* GEMINI *owners have an independence Virgoan cats respect and encourage.*

*L*IBRA
SEPTEMBER 23 - OCTOBER 23

You can't pamper this sensuous feline too much. Librans crave attention, are quick to take offense and don't take kindly to being unceremoniously shooed off a comfy chair. *ARIAN owners are good foils for tranquil Libran cats;* CAPRICORN *owners make the Libran cat feel snug and secure.*

*S*CORPIO
OCTOBER 24 - NOVEMBER 24

Passionate, magical cats with a magnetic presence. Leaping and bounding with immense *joie de vivre,* the Scorpio cat doesn't usually make friends easily but, once won over, will be your trusty ally for life. *PISCEAN owners share the Scorpio cat's insight;* TAUREAN *owners entice the Scorpio cat back to base.*

*S*AGITTARIUS
NOVEMBER 23 - DECEMBER 21

Freedom-loving rovers, Sagittarian cats lack the grace of other signs. Their great loves in life are eating and human company, but too much fuss makes them impatient. *LEO owners like the Sagittarian cat's brashness;* AQUARIAN *owners are intrigued to see what the Sagittarian cat will do next.*

Capricorn
December 22 - January 20

Unruffled and serene, Capricorn cats are rather timid with strangers. They crave affection but may feel inhibited about demanding it. Be sensitive to their needs. *CANCER owners like the settled existence which Capricorn cats love; GEMINI owners offset the Capricorn cat's tendency to get stuck in a rut.*

Aquarius
January 21 - February 18

Unpredictable, decorative and rather aloof, admire your Aquarian cat from a distance. Inquisitive, this cat rarely displays affection for humans, but observes them with interest. *LIBRAN owners understand an Aquarian cat's feelings; SAGITTARIAN owners share the Aquarian cat's unemotional approach.*

Pisces
February 19 - March 20

Home is where the Piscean cat's heart is. The lure of the garden wall holds no attraction for these cats. Attention centers on their owners, who can be assured of a Piscean puss's single-minded devotion. *LEO owners find Piscean cats entertaining; SCORPIO owners have a dreaminess Piscean cats find irresistible.*

PRACTICAL
Cat

An invaluable inventory of feline facts, from cooking for cats to extrasensory perception.

Choosing a Kitten

Choosing a kitten is great fun - but before your
new friend agrees to move in, she will
want to know the answers to a few questions!

Which Kitten?

Persians are luscious, but do you
have time to spend on grooming?
Are you happy to pamper a
pedigree, or do you want an easy-
going cat with an independent
streak? Should kitty be prepared
to spend time alone? Does
neutering fit in with your
ideals; if not, can you
cope with the
consequences?

If you decide on a pedigree kitten,
go to a recognized breeder. For a
non-pedigree, try a cat-rescue
society It is best to avoid pet
stores.

Toddlers
*Even at four
weeks, the
tortoiseshell
markings are
clearly defined.*

When you come to choose a kitten, it is wise to bear the following pointers in mind:

1 *Choose the brightest, sassiest kitten of the litter.*

2 *Look for clear eyes, clean ears and nose, sound white teeth and no signs of a tummy upset.*

3 *Make sure the fur is glossy and healthy, with no fleas, skin problems or blemishes.*

4 *Check that your kitten is lively and inquisitive, running and jumping with ease, eager to play.*

5 *Don't take kitty home under ten weeks old.*

6 *Check that necessary vaccinations have been given.*

HOMECOMING

Bring your kitten home in a sturdy box. Give her lots of love, play with her, and don't rush her if she's shy at first. She'll need a warm bed, a litter tray that's regularly cleaned, and her own bowls for food and water. Let her have a good look around before she meets any other household pets. It may take her a while to feel at home, but you will know she's decided to stay when she leaps on to your lap with a contented purr!

CAT-CHAT

Cats are consummate communicators. They use every part of the body, with subtle vocal variations, to make themselves understood. Here is a guide to demystifying feline bodytalk.

TAIL TALK

- A straight tail with a slight bend at the tip means, "This looks most interesting."
- A tail held stiffly at right-angles to the body means, "Hello. How nice to see you."
- A tail with a tip that twitches means, "I'm starting to get angry!"
- A tail waved vigorously from side to side means, "You're for it!"
- An arched tail with the fur fluffed means, "This is my territory and don't you forget it!"
- A tail held low with fur fluffed out means, "I'm frightened." A terrified cat will crouch down low and the fur will stand on end all over his body.

TONES OF VOICE

- Purring can mean, "Mmmmm, that feels wonderful," or, "You're my favorite person." However, cats have been known to purr when in pain or distress.

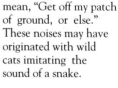

- A little chirping sound, which mother cats use to marshal their kittens together, is given by adult cats to say "Hi" to their owners.
- Yowling and caterwauling usually mean, "Get off my territory," rather than, "What are you doing tonight, gorgeous?"
- Hissing and spitting mean, "Get off my patch of ground, or else." These noises may have originated with wild cats imitating the sound of a snake.

Body Language

- Rubbing the body or head against an object is a way of marking territory. When kitty rubs lovingly round your legs, he is saying, "You're all mine."

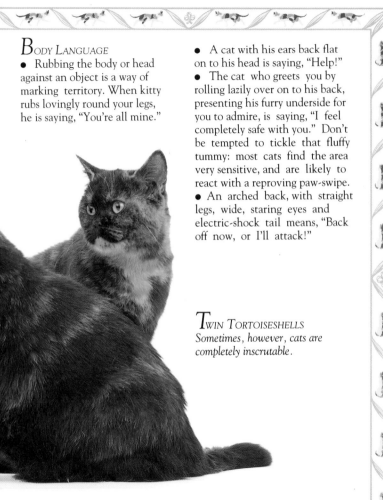

- A cat with his ears back flat on to his head is saying, "Help!"
- The cat who greets you by rolling lazily over on to his back, presenting his furry underside for you to admire, is saying, "I feel completely safe with you." Don't be tempted to tickle that fluffy tummy: most cats find the area very sensitive, and are likely to react with a reproving paw-swipe.
- An arched back, with straight legs, wide, staring eyes and electric-shock tail means, "Back off now, or I'll attack!"

Twin Tortoiseshells
Sometimes, however, cats are completely inscrutable.

CELEBRATION CUISINE

Tsar Nicholas I of Russia fed his cat, Vashka, a celebratory concoction of the best caviar poached in rich champagne, with finely minced French dormouse, unsalted butter, cream, whipped woodcock's egg and hare's blood. Rather than trouble his servants, Doctor Johnson himself purchased oysters for his cat, Hodge. It's not necessary to go to *quite* these lengths on those special days when you want to lavish a little more affection on your puss, but here are some gastronomic goodies which will tempt the fussiest feline.

Kitty Vol-au-Vent

Spoon a dainty, puss-sized portion of cooked chicken and creamy sauce into the pastry case. Top with shrimp for extra-special appeal. Full of protein and vitamins.

Liver and Bacon Bonanza

Top kitty's portion with crumbled cheese and serve warm. Packed with essential vitamins, minerals and proteins, this is a guaranteed gastronomic success.

Puss's Shrimp Cocktail

Fresh shrimps on delicate slivers of brown bread, thinly spread with butter and diced into feline-sized mouthfuls. Elegant and full of energy-giving goodness.

Drink To Me Only

Not all cats like drinking milk. Make sure there's always an adequate supply of water for your puss. Or try a tempting sip of evaporated milk, or even milky, lukewarm tea.

Mackerel Puss Pate

A dessertspoonful of mackerel pâté on fresh fingers of toast makes an instant treat for the fish-loving feline. Rich in protein and Vitamin A.

Tuna Treat

Tuna, in oil or brine, topped with crumbled cheese and grilled lightly makes a well-balanced, heart-warming feast for your feline.

Rare Treat

Raw steak or ground meat, fresh from the butcher's and finely chopped, is a special occasional food for your cat. But be careful not to overdo the raw meat content of your cat's diet.

Sweet Puss

Cats can be partial to cantaloupe, the occasional segment of apple, or even the odd sweet grape. Full of essential, health-giving Vitamin C and dietary fiber.

CAT GLAMOUR

If you are the proud owner of a Persian cat, it's essential to give your pet a daily grooming session. Shorthaired cats are better at looking after their coats, so a good brush-and-comb once or twice a week is all that is necessary.

EARS AND EYES
Clean carefully with Q-tips moistened in a solution of baking soda.

GROOMING THE FUR

1 *Work grooming powder into the coat. For best results, always make sure it is evenly distributed.*

2 *Brush the fur upward, all over the body, to remove any trace of tangles and dirt.*

FUR ON THE FACE
This can be brushed gently with a toothbrush, but stay well away from the eye area.

TOOTH CARE
Check the teeth for tartar build-up and, if necessary, clean with a brush and baking soda solution.

3 *Add the finishing touches by brushing the fur vigorously all over the body.*

4 *Shorthaired cats can be given extra shine by rubbing the coat over with velvet, silk or chamois.*

A-Z OF CAT CARE

A IS FOR ACCIDENT

Laws protecting injured cats vary from state to state. Keep your pet off the street. Indoor cats live longer, safer lives.

B IS FOR BASKET

Useful for traveling, although harder to clean than plastic carriers. Line with paper towels. Do not leave puss inside for too long.

C IS FOR CAT-FLAP

Use only where outdoors is safe. Fit at cat's-belly height and make sure it can be locked securely.

D IS FOR DOG

Cats tolerate dogs' presence in the same household and can form lasting canine friendships if they are introduced in early kittenhood.

E IS FOR EXERCISE

There is cat furniture for exercising. Cat trees can be built. Cats flex their muscles in boisterous play sessions with their owners. A few can even be trained to walk on a cat leash.

F IS FOR FLEA COLLAR

Put one on puss every summer, before he starts scratching. Check that it fits and does not rub.

G IS FOR GRASS

Cats love to eat and regurgitate it, along with any hairballs. Indoor cats should be given a pot-grown clump to graze on.

H IS FOR HANDLING

Most cats adore a cuddle, but pick puss up gently and support his whole weight. Don't grab him by the scruff or hold him under the front legs without a steadying hand under his rear.

I IS FOR ILLNESS AND INJECTIONS

Feline Infection Enteritis and Pneumonitis are the two big - but preventable - dangers. Have your cat vaccinated at around 12 weeks old and remember to arrange booster shots. Reputable catteries will not accept cats for board without certificates showing proof of vaccination.

J IS FOR JACOBSON'S ORGAN

Cats occasionally make a strange "grimacing" facial expression, with the lip curled back, when specific smells such as catnip waft past. They are making use of Jacobson's Organ, an extremely refined sense of smell which responds delightfully to certain triggers.

K IS FOR KEEPING STILL

Something a cat can do to perfection but never when you are trying to administer medicine! Liquids or crushed pills can be added to food. Or grasp the cat's head and bend back gently until the mouth opens. Press on each side of the mouth to increase the gap, and pop the medicine on the tongue as far back as you can. Close the mouth until the cat swallows. Look to make sure the medicine really has gone down.

L IS FOR LITTER TRAY

Keep it in a quiet place. Make sure it is always clean and neat. If not, puss may object and perform elsewhere.

M IS FOR MOVING

Keep kitty under lock and key while the move takes place. When you arrive, let him settle in gradually, a room at a time. Much safer to keep puss inside until you're sure he has settled down.

N IS FOR NEUTERING

Male kittens should be neutered at eight - ten months' old; females spayed at five - six months' old.

O IS FOR OBEDIENCE

Start young, and be persistent. Say "No" firmly, as you pluck puss off the forbidden chair and he'll soon start to cooperate - at least while you're within eyesight.

P IS FOR POISONOUS PLANTS

Avoid the following: azalea, caladium, dieffenbachia, ivy, laurel, philodendron, poinsettia, solanum capiscastrum, or keep them out of your cat's inquisitive reach.

Q IS FOR QUARANTINE

Holiday romances can have long, costly consequences, as the unlucky English holidaymakers who fell for a Portuguese puss found out. The prohibitive cost of importing their new love and keeping him in quarantine for the required period of six months exceeded $2000, making him an extremely expensive holiday purchase indeed!

R IS FOR RODENT

Cats hunt for sport rather than for nourishment, so be sure to feed your cat well if you want the local mouse colony decimated - a ravenous cat lacks the necessary energy and enthusiasm for exhausting pursuits!

S IS FOR SAFETY

Guard open fires; ban cats from the kitchen when ovens and hotplates are on and store sharp knives safely; unplug electrical appliances where cats might chew the cord; keep upstairs windows closed or inaccessible; lock up household poisons and keep the garage closed; beware when using irons; don't leave plastic bags lying around; tidy up tiny objects that could choke.

T IS FOR TOY

The best is often the simplest: a cork swinging from a string, an empty box to hide in, a ping-pong ball, an old thread reel, a felt mouse for pouncing practice, an old newspaper to stalk - the list is endless!

U IS FOR UNMENTIONABLE HABITS

Unneutered toms create the most pungent of smells when they mark out their territory. Even if your pets are neutered, you may need to discourage local toms from visiting via your cat-flap and leaving their overpowering mark.

V IS FOR VET

If puss has a prolonged stomach upset, seems lethargic, starts sneezing or coughing, looks rheumy-eyed (the inner eyelid may be showing), or shows signs of pain when handled, ignore any protests and whisk him to the vet straight away. Vets can also advise on vaccinations and booster shots.

W IS FOR WORMS

Most cats suffer now and then. Pills are the answer - your vet can advise on this.

X IS FOR XTRA-SENSORY PERCEPTION

Experts argue that cats have no sixth sense, but anyone who observes a cat bristle in response to something unseen by human eyes will be less convinced.

Y IS FOR YOUNG CATS AND KITTENS

Enjoy their antics while they are playful babies. All too soon they will become more sedate and self-conscious, and will save their displays of tail-chasing or shadow-stalking for moments when they think you're not looking.

Z IS FOR ZOO

Watch out for the African and European Wild Cats, the closest relatives of the average domestic puss. There is a distinct and uncanny resemblance between a tame, snoozing tabby cat and a slumbering tiger: these and other fearsome breeds, like lions and leopards, feature on a more distant branch of the family tree.

I N D E X

ACKNOWLEDGEMENTS

PAGE 10 May the New Year Prove Bright and Fair / Fine Art Photographic Library Ltd.

PAGE 11 Proud Mother by Henriette Ronner / Fine Art Photographic Library Ltd;
Pam's Cat (detail) by Ditz / The Bridgeman Art Library.

PAGE 12 Cat and Apples, from R. Caldecott's Collection of Pictures and Songs /
Mary Evans Picture Library.

PAGE 13 Interior of a School (detail) by John Frederick Lewis / Victoria and Albert Museum /
The Bridgeman Art Library; Cat from R. Caldecott's Collection of Pictures and Songs /
Mary Evans Picture Library.

PAGE 14 A Tea-Time Companion by Marcel Rider / Fine Art Photographic Library Ltd.

PAGE 15 Miss Ann White's Kitten by George Stubbs / Fine Art Photographic Library Ltd;
Exposition a la Bodiniere (detail) by T. A. Steinlen, 1894 / The Bridgeman Art Libary.

PHOTOGRAPHY: Dave King   ILLUSTRATIONS: Susan Robertson, Stephen Lings, Clive Spong

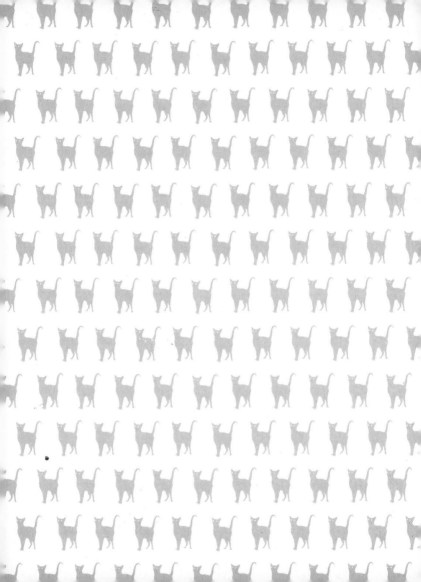